Hymns of

COMMUNITY

SUSAN R. BRIEHL

Augsburg Fortress
PUBLISHERS

SING THE
FAITH

Hymns of

COMMUNITY

SUSAN R. BRIEHL

Editors:
Gloria E. Bengtson,
Jeffrey S. Nelson, and
Sarah Anondson
Cover design:
Marti Naughton

Scripture quotations
are from New Revised
Standard Version
Bible, copyright
© 1989 Division of
Christian Education
of the National
Council of the
Churches of Christ in
the United States of
America. Used by
permission.

ISBN 0-8066-4681-0
Manufactured
in U.S.A.

06 05 04 03 1 2 3 4

INTRODUCTION

Welcome to Sing the Faith!

Welcome to *Hymns of Community,* one of nine volumes in the Sing the Faith Bible study series. You are embarking on a biblical exploration of grace through the poetry, music, and history of five of the most beloved hymns of the Christian tradition.

Hymns are the faith people sing. The lyrics are owned by the people as the fabric of their theology. Many hymns have been in the memories of churchgoers for years. The melodies and texts of hymns are often retained after most other memory has faded. This series will allow participants to connect these well-loved hymns to biblical texts.

Pastors and worship leaders spend a significant amount of time searching for hymns related to the Sunday readings, the theme, and the mood of each service. Indexes are available to assist planners in coordinating biblical texts and songs. The Sing the Faith series brings this information and its powerful faith formation capability to you.

Each session focuses on one hymn. Participants will reflect on their personal history with the hymn, explore biblical connections in the texts, learn the history and legends associated with the hymn, and consider how the message of the hymn applies to their daily journey of faith.

Preparing your study

The Sing the Faith series, designed for small-group Bible study, encourages interaction among participants to help them grow and enrich their journeys of faith. Alternate groupings, with minor modifications, would be possible. Individuals might use this resource for personal study or partner with another individual to study and correspond by phone or e-mail.

The thematically connected hymns in each volume can be studied at any time and in any church season.

The material is planned for weekly gatherings. The meeting place could be at church or in homes. The key will be finding a place where everyone can feel safe as they share, reflect, and pray together.

This study is ideal for rotational leadership. As leaders and participants discover an increased connection between worship and study, their understanding of leadership will continue to broaden. If a pastor is a part of your group, include him or her in the rotation. The opportunity to operate as a participant will be welcomed.

Adults of all ages and stages will find this study useful—singles groups, men's breakfasts, mom's time out, and new member study are just a few ideas. Because of the universality of the hymns used in this series, a young adult group may be as vital as an older adult group.

Planning each session

Gathering for the story

The first three pages of each session introduce the hymn. The instructions invite you to transition from a time of fellowship as you arrive, to gathering your thoughts about the hymn, checking in with each other, then experiencing the hymn (see page 6), and finally praying together.

Learning the story

This section provides relevant information about the text, the tune, and the legends of each hymn. The intent is not in-depth study, but an opportunity to discover stories and anecdotes about the persons and circumstances that were a part of the creation of the hymn.

Our story

Hymns and songs carry emotional and cognitive memories. In this section, you will be asked to reflect on how the hymn has been part of your growth in the Christian faith. The questions, similar in all sessions, provide time and a safe opportunity to share how the music and poetry has affected who we are as believers.

The biblical story

Unless the hymn writer indicated a specific biblical passage, the intended textual connection can never be certain. The writer of this study discovered textual connections and images for one stanza of each hymn and has provided questions to help you search for personal meaning related to faith traditions and the Bible.

Texts were selected from the New Revised Standard Version of the Bible (NRSV), but each participant may use his or her own Bible. Using a variety of translations can bring new perspectives to your discussions.

Additional questions to reflect on in this section of the study are:

◆ What is normally taken for granted about this passage?

◆ What is related to your own journey of faith?

◆ What connections to biblical and doctrinal understanding do you find?

◆ What may affect you personally in this text?

Living the story

Each hymn study ends with several questions addressing how this hymn will affect the way you live your faith as a result of your learning. What message will you bring to each day?

Each session ends with praying and singing. The closing prayer (with time for individual petitions) and singing the hymn weave new dimensions to the hymn's familiar words and images.

Experiencing the hymn

An important part of this study is the experience of singing. Whether your group is large or small, raise your voices together each week. If a piano and accompanist are available, look for the full score in your favorite hymnal. Most hymns are included in *Lutheran Book of Worship* or *With One Voice*, and may be found in most traditional Christian hymnals.

If your group has instrumentalists, invite them to play with you as you sing. Perhaps someone's hidden talent will shine! Invite a young person or two from your congregation who play in their school orchestra or band to play along for one session.

Many of the hymns in the Sing the Faith volumes appear on numerous recordings. The reference list on page 47 offers a starting place for your search. You might publicize your study in your church newsletter or bulletin by listing the hymns and asking for recording recommendations. In addition, piano collections that include one or more of the hymns are suggested on this page.

Whether you sing *a cappella* or with a pipe organ at its fullest, enjoy your time with the music, with the texts, with memories of the past and hope for the future, and with each other as together you Sing the Faith.

WE KNOW THAT CHRIST IS RAISED AND DIES NO MORE

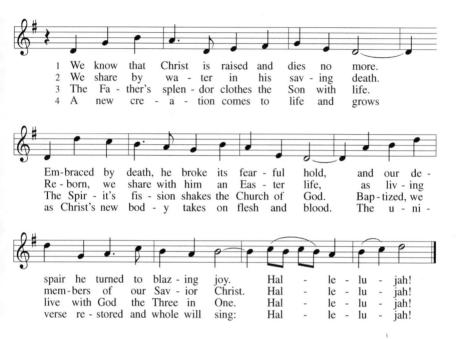

1 We know that Christ is raised and dies no more.
2 We share by wa - ter in his sav - ing death.
3 The Fa - ther's splen - dor clothes the Son with life.
4 A new cre - a - tion comes to life and grows

Em-braced by death, he broke its fear - ful hold, and our de -
Re - born, we share with him an Eas - ter life, as liv - ing
The Spir - it's fis - sion shakes the Church of God. Bap - tized, we
as Christ's new bod - y takes on flesh and blood. The u - ni -

spair he turned to blaz - ing joy. Hal - le - lu - jah!
mem-bers of our Sav - ior Christ. Hal - le - lu - jah!
live with God the Three in One. Hal - le - lu - jah!
verse re - stored and whole will sing: Hal - le - lu - jah!

Text: © John B. Geyer, b. 1932, alt.
Music: ENGELBERG. Charles V. Standford, 1852–1924.

GATHERING FOR THE STORY

Describe a time when you felt most deeply connected to a community.

Greet participants as
they arrive. Invite
them to record their
responses to these
questions in their
book.

Consider placing a
large bowl of water
on a stand near the
door where people
will enter, or in
another prominent
place in the room, as
a sign of our
baptism into Christ.

A Bible concordance
would be a helpful
tool for people who
want to list text
citations or search
for stories by key
words.

Describe a time when you felt most painfully that you did not belong to a certain community.

Invite the group to
sing the hymn (see
page 7). If you have
enough people, try
singing the hymn in
this manner:

All: stanza 1
High voices: stanza 2
All: Hallelujah
Low voices: stanza 3
All: Hallelujah
All: stanza 4

If you are able,
stand to sing.
(10 minutes)

What is your favorite image or description of the Holy Trinity? Why?

Gracious God,
> by water and your Word
> you made us living members
> of the living Christ.
You broke death's fearful hold
> and raised us to an Easter life.
Continue to strengthen us
> with your Holy Spirit, and daily increase
> in us your gifts of grace until,
> in the blazing joy of your presence,
> we live with you,
God the Three in One, forever. Amen

WE KNOW THAT CHRIST IS RAISED AND DIES NO MORE

We know that Christ is raised and dies no more.
Embraced by death, he broke its fearful hold,
and our despair he turned to blazing joy.
Hallelujah!

We share by water in his saving death.
Reborn, we share with him an Easter life,
as living members of our Savior Christ.
Hallelujah!

The Father's splendor clothes the Son with life.
The Spirit's fission shakes the Church of God.
Baptized, we live with God the Three in One.
Hallelujah!

A new creation comes to life and grows
as Christ's new body takes on flesh and blood.
The universe restored and whole will sing:
Hallelujah!

© *John B. Geyer, b. 1932, alt.*

LEARNING THE STORY

After participants read the hymn background, talk about information they found meaningful or helpful.
(5 minutes)

Our baptismal incorporation into the life of the Holy Trinity is a mystery. The poetry of hymn texts often helps us experience what we cannot know by reason alone. "We Know that Christ is Raised" speaks of dying with Christ and being raised with him to life with God. Compare that to "I Bind unto Myself This Day" (LBW 188), a hymn attributed to St. Patrick. This hymn speaks of being bound by faith to the name of the Trinity. God binds us to Christ and his "baptism in the Jordan River," "cross of death," and "bursting from the spiced tomb." We renew this "binding" every time we call upon "the strong name of the Trinity, the Three in One, the One in Three."

The text

An Old Testament scholar and a pastor in the Congregational Union of Scotland, John B. Geyer (b. 1932) has taught at both Oxford and Cambridge. Geyer drew on the ancient baptismal imagery of Romans 6 for his text, but he also incorporated language from the modern scientific world: "The Spirit's fission shakes the Church of God." Geyer once said he has been surprised that this hymn is used more often at Easter than at baptisms or affirmations of baptism.

The tune

Can you imagine singing "For all the Saints" to any tune other than the familiar SINE NOMINE (LBW 174)? Try singing it to ENGELBERG (LBW189), which Charles V. Stanford (1852–1924) composed for that text. Stanford began composing at an early age; the Dublin Royal Theatre performed one of his pieces before he was ten. Later he served as the organist at Trinity College in Cambridge and the director of the Cambridge Musical Society and the London Bach Choir. John B. Geyer chose ENGELBERG for the setting of this hymn.

The legend

While John Geyer was a tutor at Chestnut College in Cambridge, scientific research on producing living cells was underway just around the corner from his office. This research eventually led to the so-called test-tube baby. Bridging the perceived chasm between science and faith, Geyer wrote this hymn to bring the church's baptismal theology to bear on such research. Even in the laboratory, "a new creation comes to life and grows as Christ's new body takes on flesh and blood."

OUR STORY

Describe an occasion when you have sung this hymn.

You may need to adapt these questions for the participants in your group. Ask them to record their responses and then share their stories.
(10 minutes)

Do you think of it more as an Easter hymn or a baptismal hymn? Discuss.

What pictures or images come to mind when you hear or sing the phrase, "Baptized, we live with God the Three in One"?

THE BIBLICAL STORY

Invite participants to find the passages in their Bibles and record responses to the questions.

If there is time, include the image of the baptized as "new creation" in the discussion.

"A new creation comes to life and grows. . . . The universe restored and whole will sing Hallelujah!"

"So if anyone is in Christ, there is a new creation: everything old has passed away; see, everything has become new!" (2 Corinthians 5:17).

What has passed away? What is the new creation? Christ came not only to make us new, but also to restore and heal the entire universe. How could believing this reform the ways we live day by day as part of God's creation?

Embraced by death, he broke its fearful hold
Romans 6:12-14

What is the fearful hold of death? How is that related to the "dominion of sin" (verses 12-14)?

We share by water in his saving death
Romans 6:3-4

How do we die with Christ? In what ways is his death "saving" for us?

Reborn, we share with him an Easter life
Romans 6:5-8

What are the characteristics of an Easter life, or "newness of life"?

Baptized, we live with God the Three in One. Hallelujah!
Romans 6:9-11

What does it mean to "live with God"?

Determine if your group would prefer to:
◆ read and respond to all passages and questions before talking
◆ read, respond, and discuss one passage at a time
(20 minutes)

As living members of our Savior . . . Christ's new body takes on flesh and blood
Romans 12:1-8

Romans 6:5-14 speaks of our mortal bodies and our sinful selves; Romans 12:1-8 describes the body of Christ. What is Christ's new body according to Romans 12?

How does being members of "Christ's body," the community of the baptized, change the way we see and treat our own bodies and the bodies of others?

LIVING THE STORY

Invite participants to reflect for a few moments on today's conversation, and then respond to the questions. It is important to share the responses to these questions so your group can offer prayer support to each other throughout the week.

Select a leader for your next meeting and remind everyone of the time and location.

Close by singing the hymn and praying together.
(10 minutes)

Turn to page 121 in the *Lutheran Book of Worship* and read the baptismal address. Then go to page 206, the "Burial of the Dead," where Romans 6 is read at the entrance of the church. The pall is a baptismal garment. God's promises made to us in baptism carry us all the way to death and beyond.

If we were to shape our life together as a reflection of God's life, what would we need to change, encourage, or strengthen?

In Jesus, God entered human life, joy, suffering, and death. What difference does it make to you that God knows your life firsthand?

In this booklet, write something you need to confess to God and "die to" before you can fully live. Return to this later to make your confession and receive God's mercy.

God of all majesty and might,
  we thank you for opening your heart to us
  through the death and resurrection
  of Jesus.
By your Spirit, renew the covenant you made
  with us in our Baptism.
  Give us faith and trust in you alone,
  the wisdom to know and do your will,
  and the courage to live with you
  and one another
  as the community of your new Creation;
through your holy name. Amen

GRAINS OF WHEAT

1 Grains of wheat, rich - ly gild - ed by the sun,
2 We en - joy true com - mun - ion in this meal,
3 As the grains join to form one loaf of bread,
4 We shall all sit to - geth - er at the feast

pur - ple clus - ters, col - lect - ed from the vine:
man - y grains God has plant - ed and made thrive;
as the notes come to - geth - er in one song,
shar - ing bread as God's chil - dren, joined in one:

these are al - tered, be - com - ing love's own bread and sweet wine,
like the grain we are ground be-neath life's sor - row - ful wheel,
as the rain - drops u - nite in - to the sin - gle vast sea,
in this hope we re - joice as we go for - ward in peace,

now for us Je - sus' bod - y and his blood.
in the bread, like the grain, we come a - live.
so in Je - sus' one bod - y we be - long.
lov - ing sis - ters and broth - ers of the Son.

GATHERING FOR THE STORY

Describe a time when one part of your body was injured, disabled, or diseased, causing your whole body to suffer. What was it like?

Greet participants as they arrive. Invite them to record their responses to these questions in their book.

A Bible concordance would be a helpful tool for people who want to list text citations or search for stories by key words.

If you have made bread or wine, what was your favorite part of the process?

Begin with introductions. Ask volunteers to share the stories they selected, then say the prayer together.

Describe a time where you gathered with diverse or unrelated people around a table for a meeting or a meal.

Sing this song in unison, with spirit. A piano or guitar could accompany. Do not be afraid to stand up, if you are able, and move a little while you sing.
(10 minutes)

Blessed are you, O God,
    creator of the universe.
    You planted and made thrive
    many grains of wheat,
    gathered and ground
to become our daily bread.
Gather, we pray, your scattered
    and suffering people, that we might
    one day sit together at your feast,
    sharing bread as your children,
    joined as one;
through Jesus Christ, your Son. Amen

GRAINS OF WHEAT

Grains of wheat, richly gilded by the sun,
purple clusters, collected from the vine:
these are altered, becoming love's own bread and sweet wine,
now for us Jesus' body and his blood.

We enjoy true communion in this meal,
many grains God has planted and made thrive;
like the grain we are ground beneath life's sorrowful wheel,
in the bread, like the grain, we come alive.

As the grains join to form one loaf of bread,
as the notes come together in one song,
as the raindrops unite into the single vast sea,
so in Jesus' one body we belong.

We shall all sit together at the feast
sharing bread as God's children, joined in one:
in this hope we rejoice as we go forward in peace,
loving sisters and brothers of the Son.

UNA ESPIGA (c) 1973, 1995 Cesareo Gabarain. Published by OCP Publications,
5536 NE Hassalo, Portland OR 97213. All rights reserved. Used with permission.
This translation by Madleine Forell Marshall,
published by Augsburg Fortress Publishers.

LEARNING THE STORY

After participants read the hymn background, talk about information they found meaningful or helpful.
(5 minutes)

In the fourth century, Saint Augustine preached a sermon using texts from John 6 and John 15. He describes Holy Communion not only as receiving the body and blood of Christ Jesus, but also as becoming what we receive. He urges his hearers, as they are given the bread and the cup, to be what they see and receive what they are. This brief excerpt might help some understand the gift of the sacrament more fully:

"Now when you receive a communion, you receive the mystery of your own communion in love. Being many, you are one body. Many grapes hang on the vine, but the juice of the grapes is mingled into oneness. Therefore, be what you see, and receive what you are."

The text

Cesaro Gabarain (1930–1991), a Roman Catholic priest from the Basque region of northern Spain, served as monsignor of Madrid and as the Spanish chaplain to Pope Paul the VI (1963–1978). A beloved writer of liturgical music and hymns, Gabarain drew images and inspiration for his texts from the daily lives of those to whom he ministered: fishermen, farmers, shepherds, and their families. His best-known and most-often-translated hymn is Pescador de Hombres, "You Have Come Down to the Lakeshore" (784 WOV). Madeleine Forell Marshall translated both texts.

The tune

UNA ESPIGA (Grains of Wheat) is written in a ranchero style, a popular form of folk music in Mexico and Spain traditionally played with great energy on a guitarron, a guitar-like instrument. This is dancing music, and one can easily imagine the congregation singing this song as the gifts are brought forward and the table is set for the feast of "love's own bread and sweet wine."

The legend

The *Didache* or *Teaching of the Twelve Apostles*, a church document from the beginning of the second century, includes prayers and instructions for celebrating the Eucharist. Gabarain's hymn echoes one of those prayers. This prayer asks God to gather the church from the ends of the earth into one, just as the grains of wheat once scattered on the hills have been gathered into one to become the bread we share.

OUR STORY

Is this song new or familiar to you? If it is familiar, when did you learn or sing it?

You may need to adapt these questions for the participants in your group. Ask them to record their responses and then share their stories.
(10 minutes)

This song includes several images of the many becoming one: grains in a loaf, notes in a song, raindrops in the sea, children in one family. Which of these best helps you to understand how it is that many persons become the one body of Christ? Why?

Describe a time in your life when you or one you loved felt "ground beneath life's sorrowful wheel."

Describe an experience of "coming alive" like the grain in the bread comes alive.

THE BIBLICAL STORY

Invite participants to find the passages in their Bibles and record responses to the questions.

Determine if your group would prefer to:
◆ read and respond to all passages and questions before talking
◆ read, respond, and discuss one passage at a time

(20 minutes)

Gabarain's text draws upon the biblical image of the baptized as the body of Christ. Scripture bears a wealth of images for the Christian community and its relationship with God. Do you know a hymn that uses one of the following images? If so, write it down next to the Scripture verse.

1. Jesus is the true vine, his father is the vine grower, and his disciples are the branches who abide in him for life. The spirit of the crucified and risen Christ flows through the branches, producing the fruit of self-giving love (see John 15:1-11).

Grains of wheat . . . love's own bread . . . now for us Jesus' body
Luke 22:14-23; 1 Corinthians 11:23-26

What makes the bread of the Passover become Christ's body for the disciples?

Why does Paul say this is also true for the Christian community at Corinth?

Like the grain we are ground beneath life's sorrowful wheel, in the bread, like the grain, we come alive
John 12:24

How is Jesus like a grain of wheat?

How is the community of the baptized like grains of wheat?

In Jesus' one body we belong
1 Corinthians 12:12-27

What binds the many members of the body of Christ together?

How or why do the members of the body need one another?

We will all sit together at the feast
Isaiah 25:6-8; Luke 14:15-24

How does the prophet envision the day when God will gather the scattered people?

Compare Isaiah's vision with Jesus' parable of the great dinner in Luke.

2. Jesus, the good shepherd, knows and guides, protects and provides for his flock, even to laying down his life for them (see John 10:11-18).

3. Joined to Christ, we are being built into a holy temple, a dwelling place for God. The apostles and prophets are the foundation and Christ Jesus himself is the cornerstone (see Ephesians 2:19-22).

4. We are "a chosen race, a royal priesthood, a holy nation, God's own people" (1 Peter 2:9).

LIVING THE STORY

Invite participants to reflect for a few moments on today's conversation, and then respond to the questions. It is important to share the responses to these questions so your group can offer prayer support to each other throughout the week.

Select a leader for your next meeting and remind everyone of the time and location.

Close by singing "Grains of Wheat" and praying together.
(10 minutes)

Where in the world, far away or close to home, do you see the body of Christ suffering? Share with one another specific ways you might respond to this suffering.

How might the gift of the Lord's Supper shape and nurture a community to see, receive, and more deeply become the body of Christ?

How might your life change if you and your community of faith promised to help one another live more intentionally, as Christ's body that is blessed, broken, and given for the life of the world? Name the first steps you would need to take to make one change.

We praise you, O God,
   we bless you and thank you
      for gathering us into one body.
Nourish us with Christ's presence,
   feed us with the food of your mercy
      and grace, and by the power
      of your Spirit, send us into the world
to be what we have received. Amen

JESU, JESU FILL US WITH YOUR LOVE

Refrain

Je - su, Je - su, fill us with your love, show
us how to serve the neigh-bors we have from you.

1 Kneels at the feet of his friends, si - lent-ly wash-es their feet,
2 Neigh-bors are wealth-y and poor, var - ied in col - or and race,
3 These are the ones we will serve, these are the ones we will love;
4 Kneel at the feet of our friends, si - lent-ly wash-ing their feet:

Refrain

mas - ter who pours out him - self for them.
neigh-bors are near - by and far a - way.
all these are neigh - bors to us and you.
this is the way we will live with you.

Text and music © 1969, 1982 Hope Publishing Co. All rights reserved.
Text: Tom Colvin, b. 1925, alt.
Music: CHEREPONI, Ghanaian folk tune; adpt. Tom Colvin, b. 1925

Gathering for the Story

Who in your life has taught you the most about being a friend? What did you learn?

Consider having a large basin or bowl of water and a towel beside the door, as people enter, or in another prominent place in the room.

Greet participants as they arrive. Invite them to record their responses to these questions in their book.

A Bible concordance would be a helpful tool for people who want to list text citations or search for stories by key words.

Begin with introductions. Ask volunteers to share the stories they selected, then say the prayer together.

Sing this song in unison, perhaps accompanied by a guitar.
(10 minutes)

What is the difference between a neighbor *and a* friend?

Why is it so often easier to give than to receive, and to serve than to be served?

Jesu, Jesu, our Teacher and Lord,
 you poured out yourself for us
 and called us your friends.
Fill us with your love
 so that we might serve our neighbors,
 both nearby and far away,
as you have first served us. Amen

JESU, JESU FILL US WITH YOUR LOVE

Refrain
Jesu, Jesu, fill us with your love,
show us how to serve the neighbors we have from you.

Kneels at the feet of his friends,
silently washes their feet,
master who pours out himself for them. (Refrain)

Neighbors are wealthy and poor,
varied in color and race,
neighbors are nearby and far away. (Refrain)

These are the ones we will serve,
these are the ones we will love;
all these are neighbors to us and you. (Refrain)

Kneel at the feet of our friends,
silently washing their feet:
this is the way we will live with you. (Refrain)

Tom Colvin, b. 1925, alt.
© 1969, 1982 Hope Publishing Co. All rights reserved.

LEARNING THE STORY

After participants read the background of this hymn, talk about information they found meaningful or helpful.
(5 minutes)

Consider bringing a world map or a map of Africa to the study so the group can locate both Ghana and Malawi.

The text

Thomas Stevenson Colvin (1925–2000) was born and educated in Glasgow but spent most of his working life in Africa. He served as a Church of Scotland missionary, first in Malawi, then in Tamale, in Northern Ghana. Later, he and his wife, Patricia, returned to Malawi, where they stayed until he retired in 1990. This hymn is based on John 13, the story of Jesus washing the feet of the disciples. This text came alive for Colvin when he lived in community with the people of Ghana. Every day he witnessed them living out the example of Jesus, as they did for one another what Christ had done for them (see John 13:14-15).

The tune

Besides books on the mission and church in Africa, Tom Colvin published several collections of liturgies and hymns. He believed all Christians should worship in their native language. He encouraged the African Christians among whom he lived and served to sing their praise and petitions to God using their own musical traditions and forms. To that end, he adapted CHEREPONI, a Ghanaian folk tune, for this text.

The legend

In every place Tom Colvin lived and worked, he become deeply involved in the health, welfare, and development of the community. While he sat on the boards of several organizations (some of which he started), he also served in more immediate ways. He organized relief for refugees and victims of famine and initiated agricultural and health projects in rural and urban communities. Colvin's own life bears witness to his belief that Jesus calls us to serve and love our neighbors.

OUR STORY

This hymn is often sung on Maundy Thursday, when John 13:1-17, 31b-35 is read in worship. Compare this song to a more familiar Maundy Thursday hymn, "Love Consecrates the Humblest Act" (LBW 122). How are the two hymns the same and how do they differ in tone, language, and message?

You may need to adapt these questions for the participants in your group. Ask them to record their responses and then share their stories.
(10 minutes)

Many of us have a favorite hymn or song that is part of our familial or communal heritage. How might learning and singing hymns and songs from places and cultures not our own strengthen our connections to our neighbors and friends in other Christian communities?

If you have participated in worship that included foot washing, describe your experience. If not, tell what draws you toward or makes you uneasy about worship that includes washing feet.

How does what we do in worship—confessing our sins and receiving forgiveness, singing together, sharing the peace, eating and drinking together at the Lord's Supper, washing each other's feet—affect our daily way of life?

Invite participants to find the passages in their Bibles and record responses to the questions.

This song weaves together prayer, proclamation, and profession of faith. The refrain is a prayer; the worshiping community repeatedly pleads to be filled with the love of Jesus and to be shown how to serve others. Stanzas 1–3 are proclamation; they sing out the good news of Christ's boundless, self-giving love. Stanza 4 is a profession of faith, expressing a common desire to follow the way of Jesus. Knowing they cannot do this on their own, the people immediately sing again their prayer to be filled with Christ's love.

Jesu, Jesu, fill us with your love, show us how to serve the neighbors we have in you

John 15:9-17 (see also John 10:11-18)

What is the greatest sign of Jesus' love for us?

What is the fruit Jesus tells his community to bear?

Kneels at the feet of his friends

What are the differences and similarities between a friend and a servant?

How might these differences shape the community of faith?

Silently washes their feet, master who pours out himself for them
John 13:1-5 (6-12)

Exactly whose feet does Jesus wash?

Determine if your group would prefer to:
◆ read and respond to all passages and questions before talking
◆ read, respond, and discuss one passage at a time

(20 minutes)

What might this say about whom he loves and serves?

Kneel at the feet of our friends, silently washing their feet: this is the way we will live with you
John 13:12-17 (18-20)

What does Jesus tell his disciples they should do for one another?

LIVING THE STORY

Invite participants to reflect for a few moments on today's conversation, and then respond to the questions. It is important to share the responses to these questions so your group can offer prayer support to each other throughout the week.

Select a leader for your next meeting and remind everyone of the time and location.

Close by singing "Jesu, Jesu, Fill Us with Your Love" and praying together. *(10 minutes)*

As a community of servant-friends, how might you actively love one another, including those who deny, forsake, or betray you?

Identify ways your community of faith is serving neighbors nearby and far away.

Name one unmet need you see in your neighbor(s). How might Christ be calling you to respond? What is the first step you would need to take? What keeps you from taking that step? Who or what could help?

God of all mercy,
    fill us with your love
    and strengthen our faith. Open our eyes
    to the needs of our neighbors,
    bend our knees in service to them,
    and widen our hearts to receive
    all whom you give us to love;
through Jesus Christ,
    your Son, our Savior. Amen

THE CHURCH'S ONE FOUNDATION

1 The church's one foun - da - tion is Je - sus Christ, her Lord;
2 E - lect from ev - 'ry na - tion, yet one o'er all the earth;
3 Though with a scorn - ful won - der this world sees her op - pressed,
4 Through toil and trib - u - la - tion and tu - mult of her war,
5 Yet she on earth has u - nion with God, the Three in One,

she is his new cre - a - tion by wa - ter and the word.
her char - ter of sal - va - tion: one Lord, one faith, one birth.
by schisms . . rent a - sund - er, by her - e - sies dis - tressed,
she waits the con - sum - ma - tion of peace for - ev - er - more;
and mys - tic sweet com - mu - nion with those whose rest is won.

From heav'n he came and sought her to be his ho - ly bride;
One ho - ly name she bless - es, par - takes one ho - ly food,
yet saints their watch are keep - ing; their cry goes up: "How long?"
till with the vi - sion glo - rious her long - ing eyes are blest,
O bless - ed heav'n-ly cho - rus! Lord, save us by your grace,

with his own blood he bought her, and for her life he died.
and to one hope she press - es with ev - 'ry grace en - dued.
and soon the night of weep - ing shall be the morn of song.
and the great church vic - to - rious shall be the church at rest.
that we, like saints be - fore us, may see you face to face.

Text: Samuel J. Stone, 1839–1900.
Music: AURELIA. Samuel S. Wesley, 1810–1876.

GATHERING FOR THE STORY

Greet participants as they arrive. Invite them to record their responses to these questions in their book.

A Bible concordance would be a helpful tool for people who want to list text citations or search for stories by key words.

Begin with introductions. Ask volunteers to share the stories they selected, then say the prayer together.

Since this hymn is well-suited to four-part singing, encourage participants who are able to sing the choral parts.
(10 minutes)

Who dearest to you has died in your lifetime? Describe a memory, activity, place or person that reminds you of this person.

Name several persons—from any time in history—whom you have never met face-to-face, but whom you consider to be your mentors, inspiration, or companions.

What is a saint?

Jesus Christ,
    our foundation and our hope,
    we bless your holy name
    and give you thanks for coming to us,
    searching for us,
    and laying down your life
that we might live as your new creation,
    in union with God and all the saints.
Amen

THE CHURCH'S ONE FOUNDATION

The church's one foundation is Jesus Christ, her Lord;
she is his new creation by water and the word.
From heav'n he came and sought her to be his holy bride;
with his own blood he bought her, and for her life he died.

Elect from ev'ry nation, yet one o'er all the earth;
her charter of salvation: one Lord, one faith, one birth.
One holy name she blesses, partakes one holy food,
and to one hope she presses with ev'ry grace endued.

Though with a scornful wonder this world sees her oppressed,
by schisms rent asunder, by heresies distressed, yet
saints their watch are keeping; their cry goes up: "How long?"
And soon the night of weeping shall be the morn of song.

Through toil and tribulation and tumult of her war,
she waits the consummation of peace forevermore;
till with the vision glorious her longing eyes are blest,
and the great church victorious shall be the church at rest.

Yet she on earth has union with God, the Three in One,
and mystic sweet communion with those whose rest is won.
O blessed heav'nly chorus! Lord, save us by your grace,
that we, like saints before us, may see you face to face.

Samuel J. Stone, 1839-1900.

LEARNING THE STORY

After participants read the background of this hymn, talk about information they found meaningful or helpful.

(5 minutes)

Stone's original text had seven stanzas. Most hymnals omit stanza 3 and use a final stanza created from parts of Stone's stanzas 6 and 7. What are some reasons the church might choose to delete or change selected stanzas of a hymn text or alter portions of the liturgy?

The text

The son of an Anglican clergyman, Samuel John Stone (1839–1900) followed his father as vicar of St. Paul's in Haggerston, England. Together they built a church, school, and vicarage in that parish. During the last ten years of his life, he served as rector in a London parish. Stone wrote a collection of twelve hymns proclaiming the Christian faith as written in the Apostles' Creed. Of these, only "The Church's One Foundation" is still commonly sung.

The tune

Samuel S. Wesley (1810–1876) was the grandson of Charles and grandnephew of John Wesley, the brothers who founded Methodism. An organist and composer, Samuel worked to improve the salaries and status of church musicians. He wrote the tune AURELIA in 1864 for a wedding text by John Keble. This tune was first wedded to Stone's text for use at the 1867 Lambeth Conference, a meeting of the Anglican bishops worldwide. It has been a long and happy marriage.

The legend

In the early 1860s, controversy shook the Church of England. John William Colenso, the first Anglican bishop of Natal, South Africa, wrote a book questioning the historicity of the Book of Joshua and the Pentateuch (the first five books of Hebrew scripture). Bishop Gray of Capetown declared him a heretic and deposed and excommunicated him. Colenso took his case to a civil court, which reinstated him. In response to this upheaval, Samuel Stone wrote his hymns based on the creed, hoping to remind Christians of the foundational teachings of the Church.

OUR STORY

Describe a memorable time when you sang this hymn.

You may need to adapt these questions for the participants in your group. Ask them to record their responses and then share their stories.
(10 minutes)

Written to a community facing persecution, Revelation 7:9-12 describes a great multitude from every tribe and nation joining the angels in praising God. When have you felt as if you were singing with that "blessed heav'nly chorus"?

Bring a copy of the liturgy of Holy Communion to the study and note when the congregation and all the saints join the heavenly chorus in praise of God (LBW, pages 88-89).

How might singing this or another hymn give you needed courage or reassurance?

THE BIBLICAL STORY

Invite participants to find the passages in their Bibles and record responses to the questions.

The writer of Hebrews uses the image of a sports stadium to depict our relationship with "those whose rest is won." The members of the community of faith on earth are running the race in the arena, struggling, enduring, and pressing on toward the goal. Surrounding them in tiers of seats in the stands, all who have run this race before are supporting and encouraging them by bearing witness to God's faithfulness.

One foundation . . . new creation . . . holy bride
1 Corinthians 3:10-11; 2 Corinthians 5:16-17; Revelation 21:1-8

How are these biblical images of the community of Christ alike? How do they differ?

One Lord, one faith, one birth, one holy name . . . one holy food . . . one hope
Ephesians 4:1-4

The writer of Ephesians does not urge the church at Ephesus to create unity, but to maintain the unity that is already theirs. What are the seven elements of this unity?

By schisms rent asunder, by heresies distressed
1 Corinthians 11:17-22

Why can Paul not commend this community?

Determine if your group would prefer to:
♦ read and respond to all passages and questions before talking
♦ read, respond, and discuss one passage at a time
(20 minutes)

What threatens to rend asunder the church at Corinth?

The community of faith is created by, united to, and reflective of the community of the Trinity. This theme is in several hymns in this study. In the first hymn, we sang, "Baptized, we live with God the Three in One." Today we sing that the Church "on earth has union with God, the Three in One." The final hymn, "Blest Be the Tie that Binds," proclaims that "the unity of heart and mind" shared by Christians "is like to that above," the unity of the Trinity.

Mystic sweet communion with those whose rest is won
Hebrews 12:1-2

What is the "cloud of witnesses"?

How does this passage picture the relationship between these witnesses and the church on earth?

LIVING THE STORY

Invite participants to reflect for a few moments on today's conversation, and then respond to the questions. It is important to share the responses to these questions so your group can offer prayer support to each other through-out the week.

Select a leader for your next meeting and remind every-one of the time and location.

Close by singing "The Church's One Foundation" and praying together.
(10 minutes)

Why or where does the world today see the church oppressed, rent asunder, or distressed?

What might this hymn help the church remember when heresies and schisms seem to threaten its life and its ministry?

Describe a time when you experienced encouragement from or companionship with the "cloud of witnesses." How did this help you in "running the race of faith"?

God of heaven and earth,
    you promise to be with us
    through toil and tribulation,
    in times of complacency and persecution,
    whether we are full of faith
    or bound by fear.
Lift our eyes to the great cloud of witnesses
    surrounding and supporting us,
    that we might not lose heart,
    but live together in hope;
through Jesus Christ, the pioneer
    and perfector of our faith. Amen

BLEST BE THE TIE THAT BINDS

1 Blest be the tie that binds our hearts in Chris - tian love;
2 Be - fore our Fa - ther's throne we pour our ar - dent prayers;
3 We share our mu - tual woes, our mu - tual bur - dens bear,
4 From sor - row, toil, and pain, and sin we shall be free;

the u - ni - ty of heart and mind is like to that a - bove.
our fears, our hopes, our aims are one, our com - forts and our cares.
and of - ten for each oth - er flows the sym - pa - thiz - ing tear.
and per - fect love and friend - ship reign through all e - ter - ni - ty.

Text: John Fawcett, 1740–1817, alt.
Music: DENNIS. Johann G. Nägeli, 1774–1836, adapt.

GATHERING FOR THE STORY

Describe the most difficult good-bye you have ever had to say.

Greet participants as they arrive. Invite them to record their responses to this question in their book.

A Bible concordance would be a helpful tool for people who want to list text citations or search for stories by key words.

Begin with introductions. Ask volunteers to share the stories they selected, then say the prayer together.

Since this hymn is well-suited to four-part singing, encourage participants who are able to sing the choral parts.
(10 minutes)

What are the ties, negative and positive, that bind you to your family members, friends, fellow church members, neighbors, coworkers, or enemies?

In your experience, what effects can conflict or disagreement have on a community or a relationship?

Holy God,
> we thank you for binding yourself to us
> and for hearing our ardent prayers.
Calm our fears, enliven our hope,
> and set us free from sorrow, pain,
> and sin. Strengthen the ties of love
> that bind us to one another and to you;
through Jesus Christ. Amen

BLEST BE THE TIE THAT BINDS

Blest be the tie that binds
our hearts in Christian love;
the unity of heart and mind
is like to·that above.

Before our Father's throne
we pour our ardent prayers;
our fears, our hopes, our aims are one,
our comforts and our cares.

We share our mutual woes,
our mutual burdens bear,
and often for each other flows
the sympathizing tear.

From sorrow, toil, and pain,
and sin we shall be free;
and perfect love and friendship reign
through all eternity.

John Fawcett, 1740-1817, alt.

LEARNING THE STORY

After participants read the hymn background, talk about information they found meaningful or helpful.
(5 minutes)

Consider bringing a copy of Thornton Wilder's play, "Our Town," to the study. This hymn is sung at the opening of the third act. The scene is the funeral of Emily Gibbs Webb, a young woman who died, leaving behind a husband and children. Emily and others who are buried in the Grover's Corner cemetery watch the funeral from their "graves," chairs set in rows at the edge of the stage. The use of the hymn suggests that the ties that bind are stronger than death.

The text

When John Fawcett (1740–1817) was sixteen, he met the great evangelist George Whitefield and subsequently was ordained as a minister in the Baptist Church. "Blest Be the Tie that Binds" reflects the warm personal relationships he shared with his parishioners. The text also points us to God's future, when pain and sorrow are no more and we live in perfect friendship with God and one another.

The tune

Johann Georg Nägeli (1773–1836), an educator, musician, composer, music editor, and publisher, pioneered innovative methods of music instruction in his native country, Switzerland. He founded a music publishing firm in Zurich, which released the first edition of Beethoven's sonatas. His tune DENNIS was the setting for "How Gentle God's Commands" by Philip Doddridge (Lowell Mason and Benjamin Webb's *The Psaltery*, 1845).

The legend

In 1772, when John Fawcett had served his Wainsgate parish for seven years, he accepted a call to a larger church in London. After preaching his farewell sermon, the pastor and his wife were preparing to leave when their parishioners gathered around the loaded wagon and pleaded with them to stay. Mrs. Fawcett, grieved by this leave-taking, cried out, "John, John, I cannot bear this." He replied, "Neither can I." They unloaded the wagon and stayed with their community. Their decision delighted the people and inspired the text of "Blest Be the Tie that Binds."

OUR STORY

Earlier you were asked to remember a painful good-bye. Tell how singing this or other hymns helped (or might have helped) ease the sorrow.

You may need to adapt these questions for the participants in your group. Ask them to record their responses and then share their stories.
(10 minutes)

Describe your deepest memory of hearing or singing this hymn.

This hymn is often sung at funerals. Why do you think this is so?

THE BIBLICAL STORY

Invite participants to find the passages in their Bibles and record responses to the questions.

Paul writes to the church at Philippi, where the disagreements between two members threaten the well-being of the community. What is the difference between healthy and divisive disagreements within a community? Does "sharing the mind of Christ" mean agreeing on every issue? Depending upon your group, this might be an important question to discuss.

Blest be the tie the binds
Hosea 11:1-11

How does the prophet describe God's love for ancient Israel?

How do the people test that love? What is God's response?

Blest be the tie that binds our hearts in Christian love; The unity of heart and mind is like to that above
Philippians 2:1-4 (see also Philippians 4:1-2)

According to Paul, what would give a community the strength and courage to "be of the same mind" and have the "same love" even amid disagreements?

We share our mutual woes, our mutual burdens bear
Philippians 2:5-8

Whose mind are we to have among ourselves?

What are the defining characteristics of Christ's heart and mind and love?

From sorrow, toil and pain, and sin we shall be free; and perfect friendship reign through all eternity
Philippians 2:12-18

What is Paul's vision of and hope for the "Day of Christ?"

Read Philippians 3:20—4:1. What might Paul mean by "our citizenship is in heaven"? How could this "citizenship" help diverse members of a Christian community share the mind of Christ and live in unity on earth?

Describe the unity among the three persons of the Holy Trinity, the unity "like to that above."

Determine if your group would prefer to:
◆ read and respond to all passages and questions before talking
◆ read, respond, and discuss one passage at a time
(20 minutes)

In John's Revelation, we glimpse another vision of the day when we will be set free from sorrow, toil, pain, and sin: "See, the home of God is among mortals. He will dwell with them as their God; they will be his peoples, and God himself will be with them; he will wipe every tear from their eyes. Death will be no more; mourning and crying and pain will be no more, for the first things have passed away. (Revelation 21:3b-4 NRSV)

LIVING THE STORY

Invite participants to reflect for a few moments on today's conversation, and then respond to the questions. It is important to share the responses to these questions so your group can offer prayer support to each other through-out the week.

Close by singing "Blest Be the Ties that Bind" and pray-ing together.

(10 minutes)

How might you nurture, mend, or strengthen the ties that bind you to someone this week?

Name some concrete ways in which you might share a mutual woe or burden with another.

How might you thank someone who has done this for you?

Gracious God,
  we give you thanks for binding us
  to yourself with the cords
  of your steadfast love
  and promising never to let us go.
By the power of your Spirit,
  fill us with the love of Jesus,
  and bind us to one another
now and through eternity. Amen

RESOURCES

Compact Discs

"The Church's One Foundation" can be found on *Favorite Hymns from Augustana*, The Augustana Choir, Jon Hurty (Conductor). Available through the Augustana Runestone Bookstore. It can also be found on *Hymns through the Centuries*, recorded by the Washington National Cathedral Choral Society on Gothic CD49112, as well as on a Keble College Choir recording called *The Complete New English Hymnal*, Vol. 8.

"Grains of Wheat" (*Una Espiga*) can be found on *Pescador de Homebres*, Various Composers, Oregon Catholic Press, available in cassette and CD. This lively rendition is part of a wonderful collection of Spanish language sacred songs, including Gabarain's most popular song, "Pescador de Hombres" (WOV 784, "You Have Come Down to the Lakeshore").

"Jesu, Jesu Fill Us with Your Love" (titled "Neighbors" in this recording), can be found on *Hi God 3*, Carol Landry and Carol Jean Kinghorn, Oregon Catholic Press, available in cassette or CD. This is a collection of simple songs, including "call and response" and "echo" songs that are especially fun for children to sing. The meditative rendition of "Neighbors," as Tom Colvin's song is titled on this album, reminds us not to speed through this prayerful piece.